INTRODUCTION

Painting exotic animals in watercolour is one of the greatest challenges, because of their intense colours and spectacular movements. When we talk about exotic animals we think of birds with party plumage, beaks and amazing talons, of coats decorated with the most beautiful designs imaginable. Therefore, in this workbook we will deal with these animals, which have such fantastic shapes, such noble movements, such disconcerting expressions and such spectacular colours. All this will be done by a team of professional watercolourists with a variety of different skills. Some of the exercises in this workbook are accompanied by pages printed with guidelines, so that you can practise with the artist and test your own skill. Each section also has explanations and advice, so that you can develop step by step with ease and understanding. So, it only reamains for me to say, let's get to work!

AN EXOTIC BIRD: THE COLOURING

The naturalist and watercolourist David Potrony is going to paint a bird which is characterised by the variety of colours exhibited in its plumage - the bee-eater. The elegance of these birds, their varied colours and their stylised shape seem to captivate the artist. Let yourself be captivated too, and accompany the artist in doing this exercise, by turning to guideline N. 1.

Fig. 1. With a medium-hard pencil you should draw the outline of the creature lightly and precisely. You will find a sketch of this drawing in guideline N. 1. Complete the drawing, which should be lineal (that is, with no shading of the areas of shadow and without smudging with your finger). Start with some simple lines which define the beak and the curve of the neck, the head, the outline of the wings and the tail. Then, with a little orange-toned sienna, paint a first appraisal of the head and the wing, and, with a little very diluted emerald green, outline the contours of the wing. Spread a wash of very diluted sienna in the upper left-hand side of the background.

Fig. 2. To continue, now add a light wash of cadmium yellow on the head. Take a small brush and paint the blue feathers which cover the creature's chest and the top side of the wing. Do it in the same way as the artist, controlling the brushstrokes and using them to express how the feathers are arranged.

Fig. 3. At all times, keep the effects of the brushstrokes on the paper sharp. Keep expanding the colours with this typical broken brushstroke. See how the green and the blue blend on the chest and create a new chromatic value, while the contrasting zones with the sienna and the yellow appear less defined.

4

Fig. 4. The artist knows, as do you, that to minimise the graphic value of short, fine, meticulous brushstrokes would be to give up an essential resource. Now focus your attention on the bird's eye and beak. Paint the beak in colour and make the edge of the beak white by scraping with the point of a cutter. Paint the inside of the eye red, as corresponds to this type of the species. It is said that the life of an animal tends to be captured in its look, which is why you have to complete the eye, the pupil and its glassy shine with such attention.

5

Fig. 5. In such a naturalist exercise as this, it is important to keep clean the four main colours which give this bird its characteristic appearance. Don't be over zealous in this exercise: on the wing, we find green and sienna brushstrokes next to each other. These two colours are enough to convey the scale and the texture. It would be a mistake to try to add more colours, as this would create too much confusion for the viewer and make the picture too "over-the-top." Continue intensifying the shadows which outline the feathers, the chest, the wings and the neck of the animal.

6

Fig. 6. As you can see, the result of this exercise is elegant and very simple. You should do as the artist has and keep the subtlties of the yellows, greens, siennas and oranges almost intact, so that, in this way, you can create a better effect with the juxtaposition of one colour next to another. To reproduce the texture of the plumage, as has already been shown, you should paint with short, fine, measured strokes, which make a web of airy colour.

SKETCHING ANIMALS FROM LIFE

Fig. 1. Here is a series of animal sketches by Josep A. Domingo which were each completed in little more than ten minutes. To do sketches like these, it is recommended that you spend the morning practising in a zoo. To start with, we can choose animals like this koala, one of whose characteristics is to stay still for long periods of time. This will allow us to study him in detail, in order to understand his structure, his proportions and his characteristic features. Look how the head can be summed up in a circle; the ears in two triangles and the body is an oval shape. It is worthwhile pausing too see how simple these drawings are in contrast to the magnificent understanding they show of the anatomical forms which characterise each one of the animals.

Fig. 2. To do a sketch of a chimpanzee, one has to be relatively quicker than in the previous case, because of the model's movement. For this reason, it is important to find an instant medium that allows you to achieve fluidity in the drawing. The graphite pencil combines these qualities. With a graphite pencil you will be able to do the smooth features of the face, and, at the same time, have the possibility of emphasising the repeated strokes in the fur of the animal, the lines in the background, etc. When you draw with graphite pencil, the direction of the strokes is fundamental to simulate texture. Look, for example, at the vertical stroke used to situate the wall in background, the continuous but irreguler strokes of the fur which covers the chimpanze body, or the encircling strokes of the head and face which help to achieve a better impression of volume.

Fig. 3. When drawing animals you always start by drawing a few simple lines which constitute the general form of the objective: to observe the figure. For example, concentrate on the shape of this reindeer's head and compare it with that of the koala.You will see that the reindeer's could be drawn within a rectangle, while you could draw the koala's within a circle. When you have sketched the basic shape, then you should start giving the drawing proportion. For this, it will be necessary to compare distances and look for smaller shapes within the larger, general ones. From this point, we will redraw the outline hoping to get a more accurate line; and, lastly, we will do the shading.

4

Fig. 4. Before we start drawing this kangaroo and her baby coming out of her pouch, let's look for a geometric shape which sums up the ensemble; in this case, the chosen shape is a triangle. Draw a few simple lines and, when you have the structure of the animal, let's look again at the model for new information to characterise it. In this way, although the animal has moved, you already know what you want to look for. Hold the pencil lightly; the lines will still appear. They will be strokes which vibrate and which superimpose previous lines, which draw the general form of the body and the throat or the feet (because any kangaroo has to have a pair of enormous, strong feet!) Moving on, show the animal's coat with some deeper greys and, in this way, you can darken the tail and the back.

5

Fig. 5. Once you have got confidence in your ability to make sketches of animals, you can deal with drawing them in motion. To start with, look for animals like the giraffe, which moves slowly. It is not neccessary to try to convey the sensation of movement with kinetic lines or nervous strokes. Simply draw its sinuous form in a way that portrays the animal in motion. Draw the giraffe with soft, graceful lines, bearing in mind that these are organic and curving and, next, with thin strokes, draw each one of its markings. Don't worry about the rest; in following chapters, we will deal with the subject of animals in motion.

THE CHAMELEON: A STUDY IN MONOCHROME

Here is another interesting subject, a Madagascan chameleon painted by Ester Llaudet. The diifficult thing about this animal is its colouring, which is a single colour green with few variations. You will have to know how to evaluate the monochrome rather than contrast different colours. Certainly, if you want to paint this creature in the wild, the problem of movement is virtually non-existent, as, generally speaking, chameleons adopt a pose and then remain motionless for long periods of time. So, if you go to the zoo to paint exotic animals, think about choosing animals which usually stay still as your first models.

1

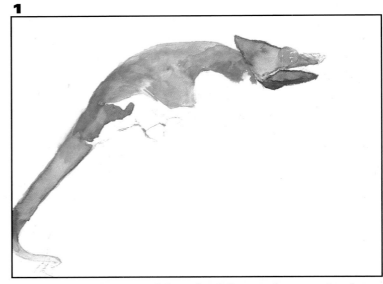

Fig. 1. From a drawing of the animal that you have previously made, in this case taken from a photograph which captures the moment when the chameleon shoots out its sticky tongue to capture its prey, you can achieve a first impression which is simple and fresh simply by adding some opportune touches of colour. You will see how the mixture of the four variants of colour (emerald green, permanent green, cadmiun yellow and Payne's grey) creates a first sensation of volume.

2

Fig. 2. The gradual introduction of new values and tones to these initial colours gradually builds up the texture and the characteristic shape of the chameleon so that, little by little, it becomes more recognisable. From now on, apply paint on dry, i.e,. when the previous wash has already dried. Add an olive green for the front foot and Payne's grey and black for the back feet and the stripes of the tail.

3

Fig. 3. Go over the body and the form of the animal with more intense colours. Paint all the stripes which cover the back and do the same with the branch it is sitting on with a little sienna and Payne's grey. Intensify the blacks and create a variety of colour by adding some touches of red paint on the crest which covers its back. Notice how the watercolour is opaque, very like the effect produced by gouache.

4

Fig. 4. With some vermilion, paint the animal's long, sticky tongue; with a smaller paintbrush, detail the lines of the eyes, head and the toes of the feet, in a dark, deep colour. You will find that when you have finished the picture, you can paint a chameleon freely, improving the details at the same time as accentuating the tonal contrasts. Finally, using an average sized palette knife, cover the background with horizontal strokes in soft blended tones, which will create an interesting texture.

A MANDRILL'S FACE: THE CONTRASTS

The watercolourist Josep A. Domingo is going to paint a mandrill's head, a subject where the texture of the thick hair contrasts with the smooth, rounded shapes of the cheeks. We suggest that you accompany the artist in this detailed, but simple, exercise which, be assured, will be very useful when painting animals which are posed at such short distances as these.

Fig. 1. Drawing the head will not give you any problems and you can do it in an umbra colour, with a firm, fluid paintbrush, in just a few minutes. However, if you prefer, you can draw it first in pencil. If you find yourself drawing from life, the first step should be to sketch it quickly, as it is possible that you will only have a few seconds to sketch the pose you want to paint. Look at how, at the end of this stage, the artist has already indicated, although only lightly, the main areas of shadow in the picture.

Fig. 2. Following the first stage of drawing and arranging, paint part of the light areas with a wash of ochre, the nose with a little vermilion (in this way, you will see the important area of white which has been left along the bridge of the nose to simulate a reflection.) Use a burnt umber shadow to intensify the mane, the throat and the contours of the eyes, so that these features are in greater contrast. With a rather finer paintbrush, paint the corners of the cheeks and leave blank areas of paper for the abundant fur of the beard, which we will worry about painting later. If you look at the top of the head, you can see how the fur is portrayed by short discontinous strokes which go over the outline of the figure. You can now paint freely and without worrying, even where two colours meet, because you can harmonise them later with the general colour and the whole face.

Fig. 3. Carry on moulding the features of the head, the eyes, the cheeks and the nose, but now add to the burnt umber shadow colour some touches of ultramarine blue to reproduce the blue colours which can be seen on the model. Paint the cheeks with the same ultra-marine blue, though more diluted, and make sure you leave small white spaces to simulate the reflections of light. Tint the beard with ochre, but for the moment don't over define it. The gradual intensifying of tones and the painting of the fur will give the picture a greater sense of volume.

Fig. 4. Complete this watercolour of a mandrill's face with some light touches, which perfect and finish the head. Also, with a few encircling strokes in the right direction, you will improve the expression of the shape and the fur of the animal. In other words, by applying a diversity of tones and shades, you will enrich the picture. Look at how masterfully the artist has done the mouth, the lips, the chin and the fur of the beard. Now, the smooth, shiny textures of the coloured cheeks, the penetrating stare and the expansive effect of the hair are clearly visible. Try to do the same. Finally paint the background with a green wash to reduce the contrast with the white of the paper.

ANIMALS IN MOTION

Fig. 1. When animals are in movement (birds in full flight, monkeys jumping through branches, squirrels running about, parrots constantly moving their head, or, in this case, a lioness jumping), you shouldn't draw hurriedly. Just because they're going quickly does not mean you have to do the same. Firstly, the important thing is to observe carefully, try to understand and study each one of their movements. When you have understood the sequential order of movements an animal makes during an action, then you can draw, but from memory, just as the artist David Potrony does here. This means that, by recording and remembering their forms, you will have the animal in front of you as a reference, even though they are moving.

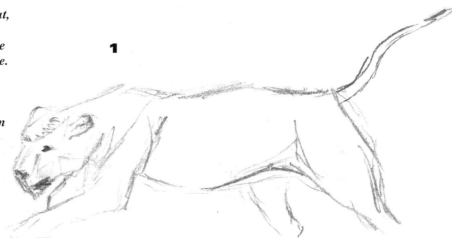

Fig. 2. Let's look at another sequence of a lioness in mid-stride and study how we should go about it. To begin with, start to draw the rough shape of the lioness with a pencil, representing her with a series of soft overlapping lines, without worrying about details or values. The most important thing in this first study is to catch the pose and portray the tension in the lioness's body. When you have got the pose and, consequently, have frozen the action, start to show some of the features with a slanting pencil, draw the eyes, some of the lines of the face and the shadow the lion casts on the ground when it runs.

Fig. 3. We are facing an ostrich which is running at great speed. As always, the most important thing is to know how to recognise the structural forms of the creature and its proportions. Then we can draw. After representing the oval body of the ostrich, tackle the neck and the head, then rub the pencil point and press hard on the surface of the paper to achieve the intense black colour of the body, as if trying to suggest the layering of the feathers. Straight away, do the legs, but leave the back one less finished to imply movement. The result is an attractive sketch, almost austere we could say, which, nonetheless, portrays perfectly the movement the animal is making.

Fig. 4. Above all, sketch the composition to capture the position and movement of the animal. Once you have understood the basic form, you can add the detail and achieve a more precise appraisal. In this way, it will be easier to understand the textures and the sizes. Start by drawing the dark tones of the animal's fur, adding deep greys. Smudge the back with a finger. Meticulously draw in the face. Finish the drawing by lightening with a rubber the touches of light on the animals neck and face. Finally, show the shadow the animal casts on the floor by smudging it with a finger.

4

5

Fig. 5. Just because it is a sketch of movement does not mean that the drawing can't reach levels of detail and perfection. Look how this monkey gives us a reference point to develop our appraisal of drawing, the proportions and control of anatomy. The facial expression is not an act inherent only to man; in animals, too, the expressions of fear, joy, shyness or anger all come with a collection of lines which define the animal's mood, through a combination of the look in their eyes, the position of the eyebrows, the way the mouth is open, the movement of the cheeks and the tension in the facial muscles.

PAINTING A GIRAFFE

The exercise I am going to do, which you can do too, requires precision and meticulousness, as I am going to paint one of the most beautiful and elegant creatures of the animal kingdom. I am referring to the giraffe. If you are drawing the animal from life, this is an animal which will not cause you problems as it is characterised by its slow, calm movements and its extreme docility and peacefulness. The only problem this exercise presents is reproducing the typical spots which cover the animal's coat However, as you will soon be able to confirm, it is not such a problem; you just need to have certain concepts clear.

Fig. 1. Use as a base the outline which you will find in guideline N. 2, or, if you prefer, draw the giraffe with a 2B pencil, but without pressing too hard on the paper. If you have problems fitting the animal in, take a perspective of three quarters on, or in profile and, in this way, you can avoid the problem of foreshortening the drawing. As you can see, although the body is in profile, it is convenient to incline the head a little to make the subject look more attractive. Next, paint the background with a light green wash, but lighter on the right hand side, under the neck. With a fine paintbrush, paint in the mane and the cylindrically-shaped neck and sketch the features of the face.

Fig. 2. Carry on and paint the spots which adorn the animal's body, at first using only flat colours (in this case a wash of burnt umber will be sufficient). The only thing you need to bear in mind here is that the spots have a tendency to be rounded on the neck and flatter on the back. Don't try to reproduce the exact form of each one of them, but don't forget the whole effect, either. It is not neccessary to be too exhaustive. You just have to remember a couple of things: concentrate on how the spots on the neck have a greater distance between them, while those on the back are more compressed. Also, on the legs, the size of the spots diminishes gradually until they reach the knee.

Fig. 3. When the spots are finished and while they are still damp, go over them with a dry paintbrush to absorb part of the colour. Next, go back over them with the same paintbrush, but this time with some water to make light and dark areas on the neck, back and legs. Paint the tail with the tip of a paintbrush in Payne's grey, English red and a tiny bit of Prussian blue and do the gentle shadows on the right hand side of the body, on the belly and on the legs, and some details on the face. Now you can consider the exercise finished.

A TUCAN: PAINTING IN A REALIST STYLE

Now we will see how a Brazilian toucan (perhaps one of the best known exotic species) should be painted in the realist style. To develop the theme, we rely once again on David Potrony. The painting process is perfectly explained in the sequence that follows. Try to follow the instructions and to complete the exercise using guideline N. 3, but remember that only continuous practice will allow you to have enough ability to tackle drawing and painting animals.

Fig. 2. Take a fine paintbrush and, with diluted black paint, paint to create the effect of featheriness. It is all about incorporating brushstrokes in the direction in which the feathers lie. This is a slow task which needs all your attention.

Fig. 1. Make a precise sketch of the toucan's outline and proportions using a medium-hard pencil. Or, if you prefer, use the sketch you will find in the aforementioned guideline N. 3. Next, paint a first colour violet on the tucan's body. This will be very useful to us in the later stages to simulate reflections. Lightly paint the background with an umber wash and, after that, the creature's disproportionate beak with cadmium yellow.

Fig. 3. The continuous overlaying of brushstrokes not only portrays the plumage in a realistic way, but also creates a solid effect in contrast with the background. The brushstrokes being so close together gives the effect of continuous lines, which are broken in some cases, leaving the violet of the previous wash exposed , thereby simulating reflections on the bird's glossy feathers. After detailing the plumage, paint the shadowed part of the beak an orange colour, the eye with ultra-marine blue, the area which surrounds the eye, pink and the small amount of colouring on the feathers in the tail, deep vermilion.

Fig. 4. With a smaller paintbrush and succesive washes, paint the beak and try to represent all its corners, curves and irregularities. Detail the claws with Payne's grey and paint a slightly detailed background of burnt umber. If you work carefully, controlling the brush, the result will be soft and harmonious. The brushstrokes which appear on the wings and the chest are short and more precise, but the feathers on the tail are not; they are freer and stronger. So, now it is finished. You should have no difficulty with the watercolour of this creature, if you have followed the method the artist used. However, you can only learn these things with practice.

FELINES

Fig. 1. *Felines typically have a round head, short ears, which are rounded in some cases and pointed in others, and long tactile whiskers on their muzzle. What is more, if we are dealing with a male lion like this one, we have to add to the list an enormous mane which grows around his face. This picture by David Potrony was drawn with a stick of graphite with which he got this rough effect by combining thick and thin lines in the lion's mane; sinuous lines in the whiskers and deep lines around the eyes, the nose and the outline of the face; and greys and lighter tones on the cheeks, beard and front of the face. Also, bear in mind the possibility of stressing lines, using your fingers, scoring and smudging. All these things give this sketch a more "plastic" and experimental feel than other drawings by the same artist.*

1

2

Fig. 2. *Here we have another feline, a foreshortened jaguar who is looking at us and coming towards us. It is a face-on study, with value and shading. Exotic animals such as this are usually characterised by their great variety of colours and spots or stripes on their bodies. When we do monochrome drawings, we cannot translate these variations in colour onto paper, which is why it is neccessary to translate colours into shades. We should make this conversion by gradations, smudging and greys. A good way to see how this conversion happens is to look at how real colours translate in black and white photographs.*

3

Fig. 3. *Here he has drawn two lions together: a mother who is licking, caring for and caressing her cub. This is a good chance to carefully study how the two bodies blend together and the forms of the animals' heads: one front on and the other in profile. Leave the synthesis of the background until last and soften it by smudging it. Studies like this, which convey the love the artist feels for the animals, his knowledge of the study of anatomy, his modeling and the excellent resolution of shadows all show what it is to draw different parts of the body attentively.*

EXOTIC BIRDS

Fig. 1. Anyone who enjoys drawing should dedicate some time to sketching birds because of their simple structure.
Birds and reptiles are some of the easiest species to draw. Look at these examples by Josep A. Domingo and you can see how birds can generally be reduced to a head, neck, body and feet. The wings usually appear to be stuck to the body, which makes the drawer's work easier. Look at this flamingo. It is drawn sinuously, so that the lines give solidity to the general shape of the body and the neck (which always looks like a snake), as well as to the characteristic feathers of this slim, elegant bird. Corresponding to its size, it has a pair of long yet fragile legs, which look like two canes with a small knot at the knees. The claws are hidden under the water of the salt marsh, its natural habitat.

1

2

Fig. 2. To draw this bird of paradise you should start by sketching some simple pencil lines which define the curve of the body and head. Continue drawing the bird's silhouette and position the wings, tail and the branch it is sitting on. Draw with sweeping lines which go in the direction of the plumage to convey the volume. The volume can be done quickly with just two or three different shades: the deep grey of the background and the outline of the branch, the medium grey of the line of the wings and the light grey for the plumage in the tail, and that is enough- be your own judge!

3

Fig. 3. It is more complicated, though not excessively so, when the bird in question (in this case a royal eagle) has its wings unfolded. Then you lose the sense of the body as one block and, instead, have a composition of more asymetric shapes. In these cases, you have to draw on all your powers of observation and your understanding of animal anatomy. We should look at these situations in the same way as we do a human figure in a pose, i.e. the situation and/or the combination of the limbs of a body make us see them in a certain way. Sometimes, we even draw them foreshortened, as with the right wing here. Well, this also happens with animals and there is only one solution: constant and continuous practice. Only through this exercise can you, as an artist, quickly understand how a creature like this moves and what poses it can adopt.

A PAIR OF PARROTS: COLOURS

Now the watercolourist Oscar Sanchis is going to paint a pair of parakeets native to the forest of South America with characteristic blue and yellow colours. When one is painting such lively creatures as these, one has to get used to making quick sketches and, if neccessary, to draw practically from memory, even if they are moving. However, don't forget to refer to your modell, the creature. Do this exercise with the artist using guideline N. 4. If you practise and draw a lot of animals you will see how, after a while, you will be able to remember their shapes.

1

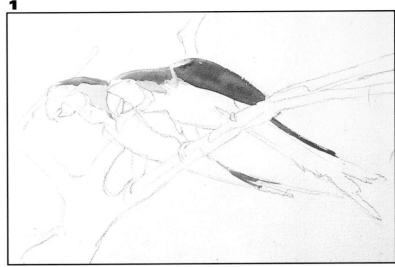

Fig. 1. Do a precise line drawing of the pair of parakeets and the branch on which they are sitting with a 2B pencil. You can also choose to use the sketch from guideline N. 4. Notice the interesting diagonal arrangement the ensemble presents. When the drawing is done, paint the crest and the wing with a blue-ish wash and add the first touches of yellow on the birds' heads.

2

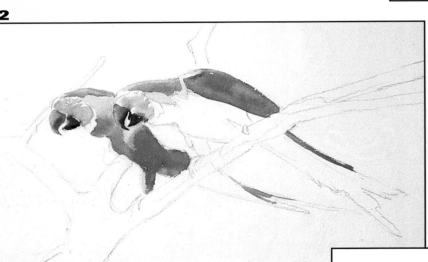

Fig. 2. Immediately afterwards, as you are working on the still damp painting, paint the play of light on the faces and the beaks with a grey colour, which you can get by mixing violet with some umber. Apply the characteristic yellow of the parakeet, although you will have to blend it with a little sienna and a touch of vermilion.

Fig. 3. Do the same with the other parakeet until you have covered the body totally with a mixture of blues and yellows. You will see how the tonal diversity of yellow contributes to creating the effect of size in the birds. With quite a thin paintbrush and with more intense colours, begin to paint the long feathers which adorn their flashy tails.

3

4

Fig. 4. Continue painting the feathers in the tail, with thick yellow cadmium and ultramarine blue. Mixing these two produces a graduation of colours with a greenish tendency. Continue with light touches, thereby perfecting and finishing the face of the left-hand parakeet. Darken the wing feathers with an ultramarine wash applied on dry and another violetish wash extending from the feathers to the feet. Notice that you have not yet painted the space for the branch on which the birds are sitting.

5

Fig. 5. Now it is time to paint the branches of the tree. Do it "alla prima", i.e. in one go. This is a technique that can be summed up as painting in one session, painting and blending the colours quickly without going back and rectifying what you have painted. Blend colours like violet and burnt umber for the areas in shadow and sienna with a little vermilion for the parts in direct light.

Fig. 6. The painting of the right hand parakeet's head does not hold any problems and with firm and careful strokes you can do the drawing in a few seconds. Afterwards, make a second appraisal of the blue-ish crests of the head and define the claws which are holding on to the branch. At this stage, revise what you have done and consider if it is a good idea to retouch anything.

6

7

Fig. 7. Once the painting of the birds is finished, paint the background with a thicker paintbrush, mixing yellow and violet washes and letting them blend with each other. Inclining the easel allows gravity to intervene at this moment. When yellow contacts violet, there is a certain greenish tendency which helps achieve an unfocused and imprecise background. This makes the outline of the "winged stars" stand out. This is a watercolour to remember and to immitate: because of its technical developement , its capacity for synthesis and its harmony of colours.

FISH

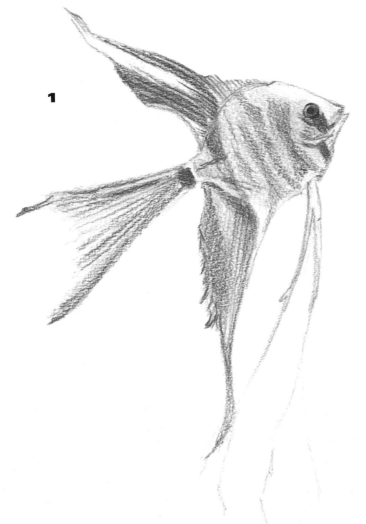

1

Fig. 1. As you already know, drawing fish has certain advantages because of their simple structure, the apparent calm with which they move and the fact that they always offer one side to the viewer so one does not need to draw foreshortenings or complicated angles. Look at this example of the escalaris fish and the following group of fish drawn by Ester Llaudet with an H.B. pencil or gradation N. 3. The fact that you are working with a soft pencil does not mean that you have to use darker tones and heavier, thicker lines. On the contrary, the soft pencil will allow you to smudge with your fingertips more easily and get a richer nuance of tones, that is to say, to stain the paper more easily .

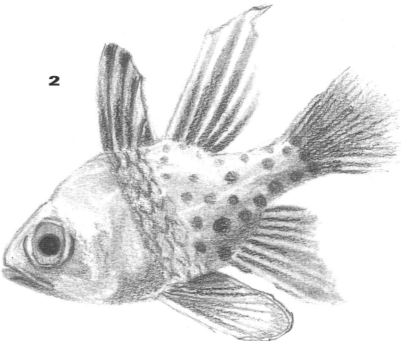

2

Fig. 2. In tropical species, e.g., this, the "pyjama fish", the most complicated thing is to reproduce the lively colours of the fish in black and white. You cannot learn this in only one session and I can give you very little advice. Perhaps, the most useful method is to slightly close your eyes. This action will help you to reduce the models' colours and to better distinguish the zones of contrast. Indicate these contrasts with variations of black and white and apply greys for the intermediate tones. Once you have done the main lines, show the reflections with a rubber and draw some details (eyes, fins, scales) with the pencil.

3

Fig. 3. If you look at this example of the common "xifo", you can appreciate the qualities and value of a soft pencil: the body has been worked in light greys (which have been smudged with the fingertips). And the fins have deeper parallels lines which represent grooves. Compare this example with the previous one and notice how the basic differences are that the body is longer and the shape of the fins is different. Whenever you draw fish, pay attention to these two things. It is these details that show if a fish belongs to one species or another and define its final appearence. If your initial drawing does not catch the correct shape of the model, don't try to fool yourself into thinking that when you apply the colours, it will make it look alright. In this case, I recommend that you start the drawing again.

Fig. 4. Now look at this tetra fish. It has been drawn with an extreme form of the technique "sfumato", that is, the absence of any lines to show, outline or limit its structure and contours. Greys and smudging dominate this technique. Look how the size has been shown by soft greys which overlay each other. To lessen the contrasts spread the colour by rubbing it with your fingers. Finally, detail the eye and the upper fin with some deep marks and show, with the tip of the pencil, the delicate ridges on the back fins.

4

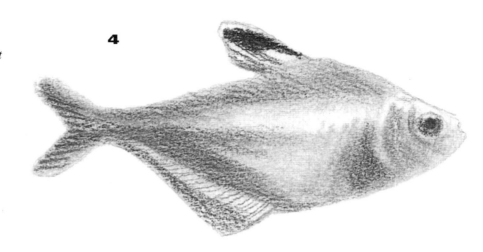

5

Fig. 5. As we have already said, the fishes' pigmentation should be translated into monochrome tones. This "Thalassoma Fuscus" fish, has a blue-ish colour with small yellow marks all over its body. When we translate this into black and white, the resolution in the pencil drawing comes from the contrast of a dark grey done with an H.B. pencil. The yellow marks can be achieved by leaving blank areas we will later work on with a hard pencil, so that they are a lighter tone. Alternatively, we can produce the marks by rubbing lightly with a rubber. To finish the picture, again with the rubber, lighten the fish's head and, with a soft pencil, darken the upper and lower fins to give more dimension to the vertibrate's body.

6

Fig. 6. This example of "Arawana" will help us see how small changes in the shape of a fish can be enough to confuse one species with another. Compare this specimen with the one on the previous page. Notice how the shape of the bodies is apparently the same. The only difference between these two is the facial structure, the size and the position of the fins. Although these differences are very obvious here, there are times when the difference between fishes can only be seen in much more subtle details than those mentioned before.

EXOTIC ANIMALS AS MODELS

In this section of models you are invited to copy them and, in this way, practise the different problems that you can meet when painting exotic animals either from life or, as in this case, from a reproduction. Here you will find an individual animal which is perfect for learning how to draw fur (*The hare* by Dürer, Graphische Sammlung Albertina, Vienna, fig. 1), a painting of animals in thick vegitation (*Tiger and buffalo fighting* by Henri Rousseau, CLeveland Museum of art, fig. 2), a suprising sketch of goats (*Cabras en Porrera* by Manel Plana, from the artist's private collection, fig. 3) and a naturalist watercolour of american birds, an example of virtuosity and precision (*Virginian Partridges* by John James Audubon, New York Historical Society, fig. 4).

1

The hare has a restrained, well-defined outline, which is only interrupted by two big ears, painted here in an asymetric way.

The details of the fur have been painted very precisely with a very fine paintbrush at the very end of drawing the hare. Look closely how the artist has used very thick white watercolour to represent the white fur.

The neutral background (i.e. it has no scenery as a reference), helps to give the form and the profile its depth.

The plane or space where the animal is sitting has been suggested with a faint shadow on the right of the picture. It is the only spacial reference in the watercolour.

The extreme twisting of the leaves and plants helps add dramatism to the scene; the fight between a tiger and a buffalo.

If we look closely at the animals and their decoration, we will see how the shapes have been drawn in a very sculptured way without obvious markings, and with high resolution.

The animal's normal habitat should also be considered; look, for example, how the shapes and exuberant varieties of vegetation in this painting transport the viewer to an exotic world.

The lack of realism helps us realise that this is a naïve work, i.e., it has a more naïve and childish resolution than photographs or naturalist paintings have.

2

3

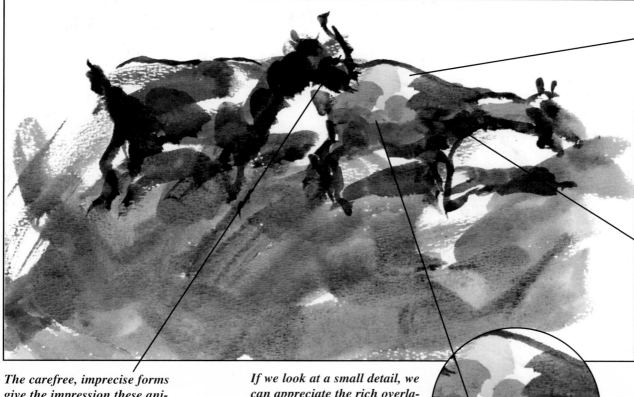

Here the artist allows some of the markings to overlap one another, he knows to keep and to use the blank spaces. These markings are what distinguish the pair of goats.

The changes in the direction of the strokes help distinguish between the planes. Overlaying one or various colours produces tonal changes; the light areas between different colours cause chromatic changes.

The carefree, imprecise forms give the impression these animals are moving. Their form itself is shown by one line which insinuates their silhouette.

If we look at a small detail, we can appreciate the rich overlaying of the different colours which have been used. If we study the picture from a certain distance, these colours blend together creating tones and depth.

If we randomly take a feather from any bird, we can see that to paint it, we will need to use different grades of paintbrush. Textures and finishes like these cannot be reproduced without this consideration.

To paint watercolours like these, you not only need to have good powers of observation, but you also need to really study and know birds. In paintings of birds, all the artist's knowledge of animal anatomy is shown.

4

If you want to produce drawings which are as realistic as this, you just need to combine a strong sense for drawing with total understanding of the pose, and careful colouring.

This painting has been done by adjusting the colours of the real model and making the colours opaque in a way that is very similar to the technique of "gouache".

FACES AND MOUTHS

Fig. 1. The different facial expressions which can be seen on animals' faces are the product of the movement of each of the facial muscles. It should not be difficult for you to understand and remember the facial lines of most animals. It is a question of looking, comparing and really studying, i.e., fixing in your memory the shape and size of the head, the teeth, jaws and the position of the most important facial muscles. When you are looking at a leopard, an impala or a bird, first imagine and then see the internal structure which determines their shape and their movements. With the aim that you will familiarise yourself with the facial structures of animals, you should copy the drawings from this section.

Fig. 2. As in the previous example, a preconceived notion of the impala's expression influences the lines that you draw. Look how with this impala, the pencil lines detail the most important details of the face in a way that almost allows us to work out the internal structure. If we compare the impala's head with the structure of the human head, the impala's differences can be summed up as a much smaller craneal cavity, a greater distance between the eyes and the position of the eyes themselves. The animal's jawbone is much wider and longer than a man's, which is why the jaw articulation is much further back.

Fig. 3. The structure of birds' facial skeletons explains the movements their faces make. Birds, with fish, are the creatures which show the least expression. This is due, firstly, to the almost total lack of facial muscles capable of changing the set of the face through moving cheeks and eyebrows; and, secondly, of course, to the fact that they have no mouth-instead of which they have a beak- their most characteristic feature, but just a bone with no expressive functions. Remembering this, copy the drawing you see here. It is a masterful example by David Potrony which is well worth reproducing.

D. Potrony

EXOTIC ANIMALS AS MODELS

Make the most of these pictures of exotic animals to practise what you have learned in this workbook. As well as trying to copy the examples produced here, paying special attention to those aspects which are detailed, you can also vary some elements, or introduce others which make the subject easier to paint.

These models offer the chance to paint a group of parrots in the tonalist style (*Parrots* by John James Audubon, New York Historical Society, fig. 1), parrots with pure colours (*With the parrots* by August Macke, Stadtisches Museum, fig. 2), a pair of roe deek painted in muted colours (*Roe deer at dusk* by Franz Marc, Städtische Galerie im Lembachhaus, Munich, fig. 3) and a group of fish done with the technique of painting on wet (*Return to the beginning* by Joseph Raffael, private collection, fig. 4).

1

The amount of detail the parrots have reflects the naturalist style of this watercolour.

The painting shows a "horror vacui" (fear of space) i.e. the artist felt the need to cover the whole picture without leaving any blank spaces.

Being a "valorist" does not mean mixing any more colours than if you gave the picture a colourist treatment. Look for example at the feathers in the parrots' wings at the bottom of the page. These have been depicted by contrasting basically two colours: sky blue and olive green in some, and yellow and the same green in others.

Wanting to show the shape better, the artist has, in this case, preferred not to paint a background; the only spatial reference is a weave of intertwining branches and dry leaves, which interwines amongst the birds.

2

The unbalanced exaggeration of colours is a recurrent theme when painting exotic birds of vivid colours, in this case, a family of parrots.

The creatures stand out from the background fabric thanks to their pure and radiant colours, which overlay the middle ground which is painted in muted colours.

The finished painting is fluid. It passes from being purely geometrical to being free in the way that the different areas of colour overlap each other.

The parrots are the central motif of the painting, however, other peripheral details have been included such as the observers in the middle ground.

3

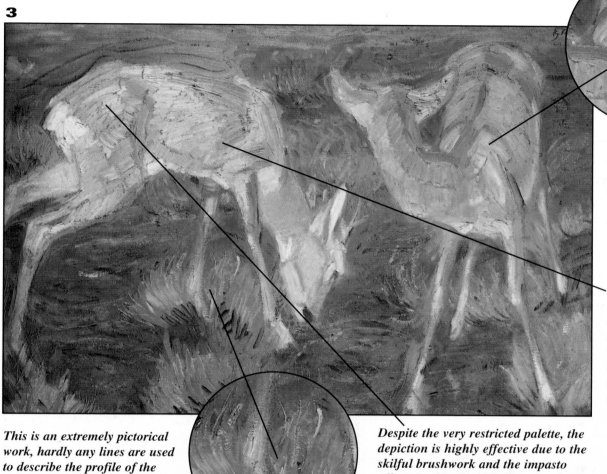

Observe in the detail above how the bodies of the roe deer are given volume through the expressive brushstrokes. Texture is of great importance in this work.

This pair of roe deer are painted using the minimum number of lines and colours. The tension in the zigzaging lines which describe the scene lend the work a solidity and consistence which make for a sound composition.

This is an extremely pictorical work, hardly any lines are used to describe the profile of the animals. See how the outline of the feet is lost in the vegetation.

Despite the very restricted palette, the depiction is highly effective due to the skilful brushwork and the impasto effect. In this case it is the use of texture which gives the work depth and volume, lending it dynamism and enabling the expression of the animals' movements.

4

In these cases, it is important to keep the colours clean and well-differentiated from each other. In this way, we avoid the picture being ruined.

Paint the characteristic texture of the scales with a mixture of semi-dry paint, applying it with the tip of a paintbrush, but without bending the bristles.

When you work on wet, the colours mix and create their own effect of varieties of colour, which produces the shine of the light on the scales.

Leave blank areas to represent the glistening of the fish and use more intense colours for the bottom of the pool, so that the fish contrast more.

EXOTIC ANIMALS

Fig. 1. Here is a perfect study of a tiger, if we consider the effects of light and shadow, the physical characteristics, the look, the jaws and the claws. It is a sketch of the head, and of the left leg which is advancing into the foreground. When we draw a sketch, the rules of proportion do not apply, so the body undergoes a deformation depending on the angle from which it is seen. In these cases, you have to look at the shape of the subject, compare sizes and reproportion the distances as we see them in the real model.

INDEX

Written by José M.Parramón and Gabriel Martín
© Exclusive copyright: Ediciones Lema, S.L.
Translated from the Spanish by Lisa Girling
Edited and distributed by Ediciones Lema, S.L.
Gran Via de les Corts Catalanes, 8-10 1º 5ªA
08902 Hospitalet de Llobregat, Barcelona (Spain)

The editor would like to express his gratitude to the artists, museums and art collectors
that have collaborated in the production of this book.

ISBN 84-89730-84-9
Printed in Spain